It´s time!

To break!
You own
rules!

Steve Walpuski

Copyright © 2014 by Steve Walpuski
Roco Verlag

1000 Inspirations for your Success

Part 1:

How is your Life... is your life right

Part 2:

How is your Job... is your Job right

Part 3:

How is your Family... is your family right

Part 1

You get what you want!

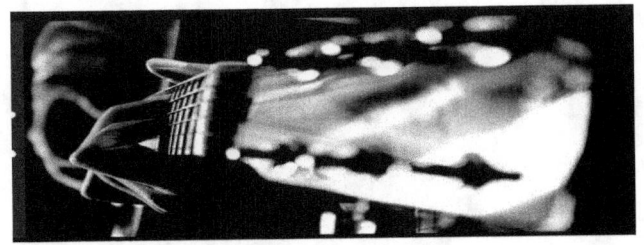

But you have to know what you want!

What is your Lifetime?

The Question of life is not easy, but you have to know, the time is limited.

30 Years = 10950 Days = 262.000 Hours

35 Years = 12775 Days = 306.600 Hours

40 Years = 14600 Days = 350.400 Hours

45 Years = 16425 Days = 394.200 Hours

50 Years = 18250 Days = 438.000 Hours

55 Years = 20075 Days = 481800 Hours

60 Years = 21900 Days = 525,600 Hours

65 Years = 23725 Days = 569,400 Hours

70 Years = 25550 Days = 613,200 Hours

75 Years = 27375 Days = 657000 Hours

80 Years = 29200 Days = 700,800 Hours

85 Years = 31025 Days = 744600 Hours

90 Years = 32850 Days = 788400 Hours

95 Years = 34675 Days = 832200 Hours

99 Years = 36135 Days = 867,240 Hours

1,000,000 Hours

.... Days

..................Years

Steve Walpuski

Every Day
Must be a
Good Day

Enjoy...
your life everyday

it's your turn
to make the best

PEOPLE WAIT ALL WEEK FOR FRIDAY.
ALL YEAR FOR SUMMER.
ALL LIFE FOR HAPPINESS.

It's time to break **your** own **rules!**

Time
Maschine

If you look into the future, what are your TOP 10 wishes?

LifeWishList

What is your lifeWish?

1............................

What is your lifeWish?

2............................

What is your lifeWish?

3............................

What is your lifeWish?

4............................

What is your lifeWish?

5............................

What is your lifeWish?

6............................

What is your lifeWish?

7............................

What is your lifeWish?

8............................

What is your lifeWish?

9............................

What is your lifeWish?

10............................

It's time to break **your** own **rules!**

Steve Walpuski

LOVE it
Change it
Leave it

Don't believe in something,
and you have to know
lifetime is limited and you
have to look what's up
around you, do you feel
realy good an everything
gives you that what you need
for a good life.

"
Don't wait for the right person to come into your
life. Make yourself the right person to walk into
someone else's life.

Start
FIGHT & WIN

Success KILLER are

everywhere

Who are successkiller?

Friends, Family, <u>Colleague</u> at work &

Yourself

The future belongs to those who believe in the beauty of their dreams.

Eleanor Roosevelt (1884-1962)

What is the structur of your life?

Love &

Passion

to your life...

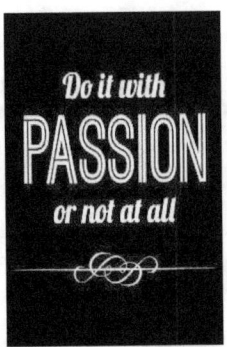

is this the right way

Find the job you love

1: Identify your greatest passion. Use these questions to help you:
If I could accomplish one thing in my life, it would be.
If I could make an important contribution in my work, it would be...

2: Identify three things you can do each day to bring your passion into the work you do.

3: Explore what you need in order to sustain your passion. Is that a secondary income, more time to think, or paying closer attention to relationships?

POSSIBLE

Causality

The reason of succsess
Is between

Cause &
effect

You cause love

You get love

You cause ...

You get ...

You cause ...

You get ...

You cause ...

You get ...

THE Rules of Life

7 RULES OF LIFE

1) Make peace with your past so it won't screw up the present.
2) What others think of you is none of your business.
3) Time heals almost everything, give it time.
4) Don't compare your life to others and don't judge them. You have no idea what their journey is all about.
5) Stop thinking too much, it's alright not to know the answers. They will come to you when you least expect it.
6) No one is in charge of your happiness, except you.
7) Smile. You don't own all the problems

Concentration on your

Target

Do you know and love your aim?

Focus on Success

1. What will you do?
2. What can you do?
3. When will you start?

Wish – Plan
Risk
–
Triumph

Your Masterplan

Please go back to the **wishList** on page 10 and write all wishes that you have down, please write it down...

All big **Stars** have a visionboard, and now you have also an visionboard.

Steve Walpuski

You are the

architect

of your life!

Magic Words

Nerves of Steal

To conquer resitance

Quick-wittedness

Rules of suggestion

Persuasiveness

Trust

STOP WISHING
START DOING!

The day I will stop loving you, is the day i will close my eyes forever!

Steve Walpuski

What is your motivation?

Every motivation needs

an

MOTIV

Steve Walpuski

We must learn to kiss!

K.I.S.S. - Keep it Short & Simple

Even better: K.I.S.S.S. - Keep it Short, Simple and Specific

We need to
communicate our

main message in

short, simple & specific

ways

Steve Walpuski

APLOMB

Don't   wait   until
everything is perfect!

It's all the time a
challenge!

It doesn't matter,
start right now, you
will get stronger with
each single step you
go

Steve Walpuski

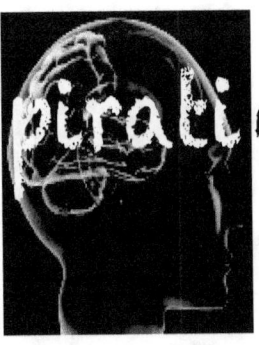

Inspiration

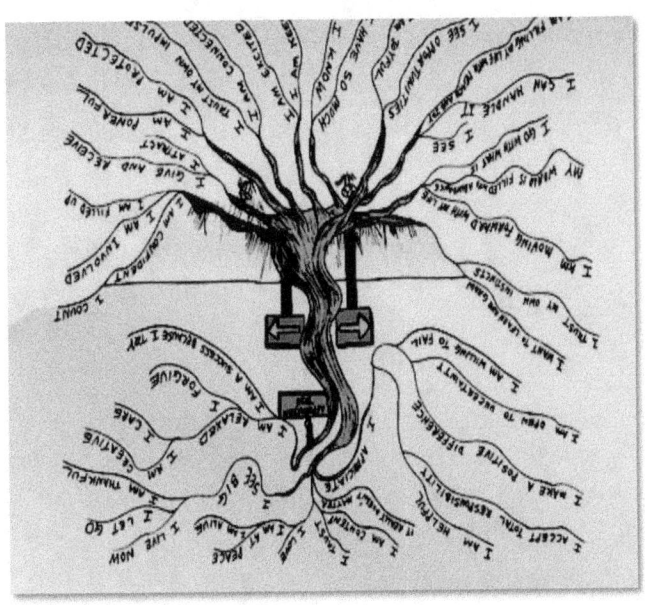

Take only your interests

Steve Walpuski

Expert your knowledge

USE YOUR BRAIN

Experience

Expert knowledge

Steve Walpuski

Your World is bigger
than you can

imagine

œkqweqeqeewdjdfvdflbk
adfladfjaksdfhadsklädf
v#sdlvjaskrfkhsdjvdhvj
kdhvsdäjfhadasdjyfhdkf
jastffgjhdfjhfsdlfjadläg
kgagf8uifoajdgfaf86dft
asgdfudagfaus6dfztasdf
uökjrthegöufdgöaiughk
adfgasdfzhöbgäaedhfga
sjkdtgahwsdgfaeeskdgjh
airpzgufazeufgiaeginaeg
haitheaöegaheiguöakehg
daufzgdfölhfäaeehfufjhi
2344hwi4tjrwöhdkJDFG
jdhföshDNFhlgökHSDFeHJ
ASHDGFÖKAmnbvruhgfΩ

Somebody who wants to be successful need to know.

YOU cAN learn to BE

SUCCESSFUL!

Take as example your successful Personal Ideal!

Copy them!

WHEN NOTHING GOES RIGHT - GO LEFT!

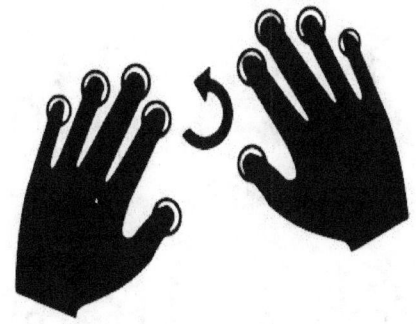

positiv
thinking

Success is dissolving

PROBLEMS...

Do you know the problems of your costumers.

Problem = Chance

YOU Have to

KILL your # # # # . .

1. Inside resistance
2. Outside resistance
3. ANGST – Fear
4. Doubt
5. Inferiority –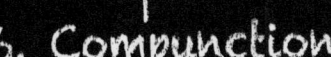
   complex
6. Compunction

Steve Walpuski

 Passion for you

Get a free Human

Trust//self confidence// speak with feeling //you have successful friends//lust for life//be satisfied//search for experience// have courage//be happy//be successful//

Statistics make 7 of 10 Dessicions right

Thanks for buying
this book...

It will crow from
know on to a 1000
pages inspiration
book for more
success in your

LIFE...

Steve

All you need in this life is ignorance and
confidence, and then success is sure.

Mark Twain

Ability is nothing without opportunity.

Napoleon Bonaparte

If you can't stand the heat, get out of the kitchen.

Harry S. Truman

The world is full of willing people, some willing to work, the rest willing to let them.

Robert Frost

Treat people as if they were what they ought to be
and you help them to become what they are
capable of being.

Johann Wolfgang von Goethe

Nothing is paticularily hard if you divide it into small jobs.

Henry Ford

In skating over thin ice, our safety is in our speed..

Ralph Waldo Emerson

If you can dream it, you can do it.

Walt Disney

Business? That's very simple: it's other people's money.

Alexandre Dumas

The man who is swimming against the stream
knows the strength of it.

Woodrow Wilson

The hardest thing is to take less when you can get more.

Frank Mc Kinney Hubbard

Never hire someone who knows less than you do
about what he's hired to do.

Malcolm Forbes

The prize of greatness is responsibility.

Winston Churchill

There is no useful rule without an exception.

Thomas Fuller

Great ideas need landing gear as well as wings.

C.D. Jackson

Daring ideas are like chessmen moved forward.
They may be beaten, but they may start a winning
game.

Johann Wolfgang von Goethe

Always remember that this whole thing was
started by a mouse.

Walt Disney

To succeed in business it is necessary to make others see things as you see them.

John H. Patterson

It is not enough to be busy; so are the ants.
The question is: What are we busy about?

Henry David Thoreau

No grand idea was ever born in a conference, but a lot of foolish ideas have died there.

F. Scott Fitzgerald

Genius begins great works, labor alone finishes them.

Joseph Joubert

True friends stab you in the font.

Oscar Wilde

Well done is better than well said.

Benjamin Franklin

All men by nature desire knowledge.

Aristoteles

It is either easy or impossible.

Salvador Dalí

If you are out to describe the truth, leave the
elegance to the tailor.

Albert Einstein

In order to write about life, first you must live it.

Ernest Hemingway

Everything you can imagine is real.

Pablo Picasso

It is not where you start but how high you aim that matters for success.

Nelson Mandela

Men of few words are the best men.

William Shakespeare

A thing is not necessarily true because a man
dies for it.

Oscar Wilde

Buy land, they're not making it anymore.

Mark Twain

I am not young enough to know everything.

Oscar Wilde

We don't grow older, we grow riper.

Pablo Picasso

The shortest answer is doing the thing.

Ernest Hemingway

Those who do not want to imitate anything,
produce nothing.

Salvador Dalí

Happy is he who causes a scandal.

Salvador Dalí

You never fail until you stop trying.

Albert Einstein

Bad artists copy. Good artists steal.

Pablo Picasso

Nothing will come of nothing.

William Shakespeare

Every saint has a past and every sinner has a future.

Oscar Wilde

"Classic." A book which people praise and don't read.

Mark Twain

A friend is a second self.

Aristoteles

I don't do drugs. I am drugs.

Salvador Dalí

Information is not knowledge.

Albert Einstein

I like to listen. I have learned a great deal from listening carefully. Most people never listen.

Ernest Hemingway

Youth has no age.

Pablo Picasso

Better a broken promise than none at all.

Mark Twain

I can resist everything except temptation.

Oscar Wilde

It always seems impossible until its done.

Nelson Mandela

Imagination is more important than knowledge.

Albert Einstein